Houghton Mifflin Harcourt
Physics

Performance Expectations Guide

Houghton Mifflin Harcourt™

Contents

Performance Expectations Guide

Introduction

The Next Generation Science Standards (NGSS) include Performance
Expectations for physics that state what you should know and be able to
do by the end of the course. This guide provides activities to help you
prepare to meet the standards.

For each Performance Expectation, you will find a Challenge Activity
that is posed as a performance task—a lab or an investigation, a research
project, or another activity. The task addresses the Performance Expectation. The Challenge Activity will provide some guidance, such as back-
ground information, materials to use, questions to consider, and tips for
completing the challenge successfully.

Physics Performance Expectations

Motion and Stability: Forces and Interactions

HS-PS2-1 Analyze data to support the claim that Newton's second law of motion describes the mathematical relationship among the net force on a macroscopic object, its mass, and its acceleration.

HS-PS2-2 Use mathematical representations to support the claim that the total momentum of a system of objects is conserved when there is no net force on the system.

HS-PS2-3 Apply scientific and engineering ideas to design, evaluate, and refine a device that minimizes the force on a macroscopic object during a collision.*

HS-PS2-4 Use mathematical representations of Newton's Law of Gravitation and Coulomb's Law to describe and predict the gravitational and electrostatic forces between objects.

HS-PS2-5 Plan and conduct an investigation to provide evidence that an electric current can produce a magnetic field and that a changing magnetic field can produce an electric current.

Energy

HS-PS3-1 Create a computational model to calculate the change in the energy of one component in a system when the change in energy of the other component(s) and energy flows in and out of the system are known.

HS-PS3-2 Develop and use models to illustrate that energy at the macroscopic scale can be accounted for as a combination of energy associated with the motions of particles (objects) and energy associated with the relative positions of particles (objects).

HS-PS3-3 Design, build, and refine a device that works within given constraints to convert one form of energy into another form of energy.*

HS-PS3-4 Plan and conduct an investigation to provide evidence that the transfer of thermal energy when two components of different temperature are combined within a closed system results in a more uniform energy distribution among the components in the system (second law of thermodynamics).

HS-PS3-5 Develop and use a model of two objects interacting through electric or magnetic fields to illustrate the forces between objects and the changes in energy of the objects due to the interaction.

*denotes the integration of traditional science content with an engineering practice

Physics Performance Expectations

Waves and Their Applications in Technologies for Information Transfer

HS-PS4-1   Use mathematical representations to support a claim regarding relationships among the frequency, wavelength, and speed of waves traveling in various media.

HS-PS4-2   Evaluate questions about the advantages of using a digital transmission and storage of information.

HS-PS4-3   Evaluate the claims, evidence, and reasoning behind the idea that electromagnetic radiation can be described either by a wave model or a particle model, and that for some situations one model is more useful than the other.

HS-PS4-4   Evaluate the validity and reliability of claims in published materials of the effects that different frequencies of electromagnetic radiation have when absorbed by matter.

HS-PS4-5   Communicate technical information about how some technological devices use the principles of wave behavior and wave interactions with matter to transmit and capture information and energy.*

Engineering Design

HS-ETS1-1   Analyze a major global challenge to specify qualitative and quantitative criteria and constraints for solutions that account for societal needs and wants.

HS-ETS1-2   Design a solution to a complex real-world problem by breaking it down into smaller, more manageable problems that can be solved through engineering.

HS-ETS1-3   Evaluate a solution to a complex real-world problem based on prioritized criteria and trade-offs that account for a range of constraints, including cost, safety, reliability, and aesthetics, as well as possible social, cultural, and environmental impacts.

HS-ETS1-4   Use a computer simulation to model the impact of proposed solutions to a complex real-world problem with numerous criteria and constraints on interactions within and between systems relevant to the problem.

*denotes the integration of traditional science content with an engineering practice

Name _____ Class _____ Date _____

HS-PS2-1: Force, Mass, and Acceleration

HS-PS2-1 Analyze data to support the claim that Newton's second law of motion describes the mathematical relationship among the net force on a macroscopic object, its mass, and its acceleration.

Challenge Activity

Challenge: Analyze experimental data related to force, mass, and acceleration and compare the mathematical relationships observed with those described by Newton's second law.

Newton's second law states that any net external force applied to a mass causes the mass to accelerate according to a specific equation. In this activity, you will examine data generated by an animation simulating how force, mass, and acceleration are related for a sailboat.

Use the simulation mechanism to observe how different factors, such as those shown in the diagram, affect a sailboat. Design an experiment and gather data for different conditions, changing one variable at a time.

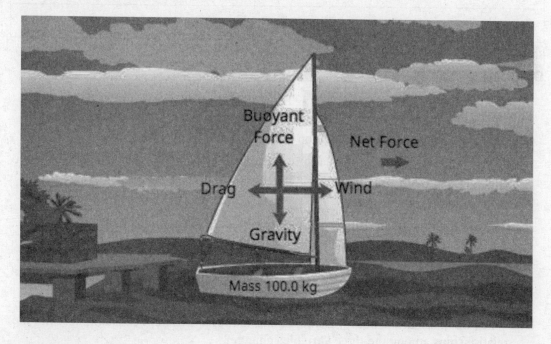

MATERIALS

- computer with Internet access
- materials to complete the extension laboratory activity, as necessary

HS-PS2-1: Force, Mass, and Acceleration *continued*

MEET THE CHALLENGE

1. Access the Section 4.3 Animated Physics: Force. Using the information provided on the Introduction screen of the animation, draw a diagram of the simulation setup, identifying factors that affect the sailboat's motion.

2. Move to the Feature tab of the Animated Physics activity. Design a series of trials using the simulation to determine how mass and force affect the boat's acceleration. Change either the mass or the force in each trial.

3. Record the values you used for variables in each trial and record the data generated.

Trial	Boat Mass (kg)	Net Force (F_{net})	Acceleration (m/s^2)
1			
2			
3			
4			
5			
6			

DOCUMENTATION

1. Write down the procedure you used to generate your data and create a report that includes the following:
   - a diagram of the sailboat simulation setup
   - a description of the experimental procedure, including what variables were changed and what variables were held constant for each trial
   - the data table you generated

2. **Analyze** Describe in words the relationship observed between the force, mass, and acceleration data gathered in each trial. Describe in words how changing each variable in isolation affected the other variables.
   - When the force was altered and mass was kept constant, how did the relationships among the three variables change?
   - When the mass of the boat was altered and the force was kept constant, how did the relationships among the three variables change?

3. Using **F** for force, *m* for mass, and **a** for acceleration, write an equation that describes the relationships among the three variables.

4. **Extension** Design an experimental setup that you could use to test the relationship between force, mass, and acceleration in the laboratory. Indicate required materials and, if requested by your teacher, create the setup and perform the experiment.

Motion and Stability: Forces and Interactions

HS-PS2-2: Momentum Conservation

HS-PS2-2 Use mathematical representations to support the claim that the total momentum of a system of objects is conserved when there is no net force on the system.

Challenge Activity

Challenge: Experimentally verify that momentum is conserved in collisions between objects.

Every object in motion has momentum. When objects collide, the momentum of the objects changes, as shown in the images below. Your goal will be to verify that momentum is conserved during both elastic and perfectly inelastic collisions.

- Elastic collisions occur when objects bounce off one another.
- Perfectly inelastic collisions occur when objects stick together and move as one object after the collision.

In this lab, you will design an experiment using dynamics carts to determine whether momentum is conserved in both elastic and perfectly inelastic collisions.

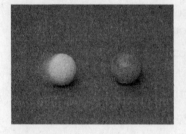  

MATERIALS
- balance
- calculator
- dynamics cart track
- dynamics carts with hook and loop fasteners or magnetic attachments (2)
- meter sticks
- probeware such as motion detectors or photogates (optional)
- stopwatches

SAFETY
- Make sure to catch dynamics carts before they go off the track or contact any probeware.

MEET THE CHALLENGE

1. Develop an experiment or a set of experiments that will determine whether momentum is conserved in both elastic and perfectly inelastic collisions.

2. Write a procedure for your experiment. As you plan the procedure, make the following decisions:

   - Decide how you will measure the momentum of the carts before and after the collision.

   - Select the materials and technology that you will need for your experiment. If you have materials you would like to use in addition to those provided, discuss your idea with your teacher.

3. Have your teacher approve your plans.

4. Obtain your materials and set up any apparatus you will need.

5. Collect data and organize the information in appropriate tables, graphs, and/or charts. Be certain that the tables, graphs, and charts are properly constructed and labeled.

TIPS

- Consider what you know about elastic and inelastic collisions. Think about what variables affect the momentum of an object and how you could best control for these variables. What are ways that you can minimize error in your measurements?

- Identify and record the criteria and constraints of the challenge. Be sure to follow any guidelines that your teacher may provide.

- Diagram the system and consider how it will change from the time of the initial state.

- The momentum of an object is given by the equation $p = mv$.

DOCUMENTATION

1. Describe how your experiment addresses the challenge.

2. **Summarizing Data** Summarize your findings and observations and analyze any data tables, charts, or graphs that you created. Include the following:

   - the data and related calculations that display whether momentum was conserved in your experiment

   - the summary of your findings and observations

3. **Discussion** Consider the ramifications of your findings. What does it mean for momentum to be conserved? Think about how your experiment could have been improved:

   - What are the main differences between the two types of collisions? Considering that momentum is not being lost in either collision, what properties might be different in an elastic and an inelastic collision?

   - How could your experiment have been improved to produce more accurate and precise results? What were some inherent sources of error in your experiment?

Motion and Stability: Forces and Interactions

HS-PS2-3: Egg Drop Challenge

HS-PS2-3 Apply scientific and engineering ideas to design, evaluate, and refine a device that minimizes the force on a macroscopic object during a collision.*

*denotes the integration of traditional science content with an engineering practice

Challenge Activity

Challenge: Design, within constraints, a device to minimize the force on an egg dropped to the ground from a great height.

Cars, sports equipment, and other equipment are constantly changing as new materials and designs provide safety advantages over previous designs. No matter what materials or designs are being used, the scientists, engineers, and designers who create safety devices must understand the basic physics involving forces and motion, such as Newton's laws of motion. In this activity, use your knowledge of physics to create a device to protect an uncooked egg dropped from a height.

MATERIALS

- assortment of materials, such as toothpicks, glue, fabric, rubber bands, cotton balls, and others (based on specific design criteria)
- equipment to measure height of drop and mass of egg
- other laboratory equipment as needed
- uncooked egg

SAFETY

- Exercise caution when dropping the egg from a height. Your teacher will inform you of the guidelines and rules for the specific location.
- Perform this experiment in a clear area and remain at least 5 m away from the drop site during a drop. Place a tarp on the ground where the eggs will be dropped. Do not walk or stand on the tarp.

| HS-PS2-3: Egg Drop Challenge *continued*

MEET THE CHALLENGE

1. Use at least one engineering design cycle to design, test, and revise a device to meet the challenge. You can use the tips provided as you wish. You may need to submit your design for review before building the first version or making major changes.

2. Develop supporting material describing your device, including an accurate visual of your final design and evidence that your design meets the challenge consistently.

3. Your teacher may require peer review of designs or request that you produce additional items, such as instructions for use.

4. Address the items listed in the Documentation section, and be prepared to demonstrate your design.

TIPS

- Identify and record the criteria and constraints of the challenge. Be sure to follow any design guidelines that your teacher may provide.

- Review the materials and options provided for the challenge. What factors can you change easily to adjust the design of your device? Which changes are likely to help you meet the challenge? After you've completed your first tests, try adjusting these factors individually to improve your results.

- Use your understanding of physics to guide your design. Identify the variables that affect the force acting on an object in a collision, and determine how to adjust your design to minimize the force acting on the egg. In your notes, explain how your choices in materials and design affect the variables you've identified.

DOCUMENTATION

1. Provide evidence of how your design addresses the challenge. Include test results from your final design. Evaluate how well your device protected the egg.

2. **Features** Identify the main features of your design and the purpose of each. Include the following:
   - a description of how the materials you chose affected the forces acting on the egg
   - an analysis, including a labeled diagram showing the important features of your design, of how your design affected the forces acting on the egg
   - a scientific explanation of how these features minimized the force of the collision

3. **Testing** Describe the testing process and how you changed your design based on the results of your tests.

4. **Tradeoffs** Identify any criteria or constraints that are not fully addressed by your design, along with any tradeoffs you made.

Motion and Stability: Forces and Interactions

HS-PS2-4: Coulomb's Law and Field Forces

HS-PS2-4 Use mathematical representations of Newton's Law of Gravitation and Coulomb's Law to describe and predict the gravitational and electrostatic forces between objects.

Challenge Activity

Challenge: Measure the relationship between conduction, charge, and movement, and relate these to Coulomb's law.

Buildup of static electricity is a normal, everyday occurrence. Although it may be annoying to get zapped by your car door handle or to have frizzy hair, it is not dangerous. Consider, however, what could happen if the static electricity accumulates in a gasoline can at a filling station. The spark that would be generated when the static electricity discharged could ignite the gasoline vapors and cause an explosion.

That's exactly what happened to an unsuspecting motorist in Las Vegas in 2002. The man set his portable gasoline can in the plastic-lined bed of his pickup truck. As gasoline sloshed into the can, electric charge built up. The plastic bed liner acted as an insulator that prevented the charge from running into the ground. Without warning, a spark jumped back to the gasoline nozzle, causing a fire that seriously injured the motorist.

Static electricity has many effects, from shorted electronic devices to lightning. How does a buildup of static electricity create an electric field like the one demonstrated in the image below? How does the electric force affect the movement of an object? How can you relate Coulomb's law to what you observe in the lab?

HS-PS2-4: Coulomb's Law and Field Forces *continued*

MATERIALS

- fur swatch, paper, and adhesive tape
- metal and rubber rods
- polystyrene balls, coated in metallic paint
- protractor and ruler
- ring stand and ring clamp
- scissors, thread, sewing needles, thimble, and magnetic needle keeper
- teacher-provided additional materials, such as rods of various materials and scraps of different cloths or furs

SAFETY

- Wear safety goggles and an apron at all times.
- Use a thimble to protect against punctures by the needle. Your teacher can demonstrate a safe way to use the needle to set up the equipment.

MEET THE CHALLENGE

1. Form a hypothesis about the factors that might determine how a charged rod affects a suspended ball. Develop an experiment that will identify the variables that affect the interactions between the ball and the rod. Limit the number of conditions to those that can be completed during the time allotted for this lab. Consult with your teacher to make sure that the conditions you have chosen are appropriate.

2. Plan and write a procedure for your experiment, including which variables you will include, what will serve as your control, and what materials and technology you will need in addition to those your teacher has provided. Have your teacher approve your plans.

3. Obtain your materials and set up any apparatus you will need. Take appropriate safety precautions. Make objective observations and collect data. Organize the information in appropriate tables and/or graphs that are properly constructed and labeled.

TIPS

- Experiment with rubbing each rod against different materials to build up different amounts of charge. Conduct tests to determine how to increase the amount of charge and how to compare or measure the results.

- Once a charge has been built up, make sure the charged object does not touch any conductors, including your hands. One way to protect the ball from touch is to use a needle to thread a string through the ball and suspend the ball from a ring stand.

- Once the ball is suspended, tape a ruler and a sheet of paper to the ring stand behind the ball to measure the distance the ball moves when the charged rod is brought near it. Observe how the distance moved by the ball changes as you move the rod closer to the ball. Repeat the procedure with increasing amounts of charge on the rod.

| HS-PS2-4: Coulomb's Law and Field Forces *continued*

DOCUMENTATION

1. Summarize your findings and observations. Include an analysis of any data tables or graphs that you produced.

2. **Evaluating Models** Was your experiment a good model for identifying and demonstrating the factors that affect the strength of an electric field? Explain why or why not and give examples of what might be missing from your model.

3. **Analysis** Describe how well your results matched your predictions. Share your results with your classmates. Which hypotheses were supported? What conclusions can you draw from your results? From class results?

4. **Making Connections** Do your results support Coulomb's law? Use evidence from your investigation to explain your answer. Apply what you learned about field forces in this activity to other types of field forces, such as gravitational force. Describe the relationship you would expect to find between gravitational force and distance for two objects, such as two planets or a planet and one of its satellites.

HS-PS2-5: Electric Currents and Magnetic Fields

HS-PS2-5 Plan and conduct an investigation to provide evidence that an electric current can produce a magnetic field and that a changing magnetic field can produce an electric current.

Challenge Activity

Challenge: Use provided equipment to show that a magnetic field, such as the one evidenced in the image below, can be produced from an electric current and that a changing magnetic field can produce an electric current.

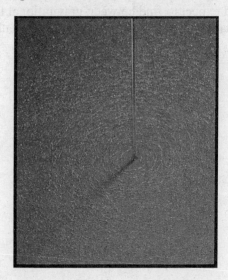

Your teacher will provide you with an assortment of equipment such as that listed. You will plan and carry out an investigation or a set of investigations of the relationships between electric currents and magnetic fields. Your plan should include descriptions and diagrams of the apparatus you will use, the steps of the procedure you will follow, and the observations and the measurements you will record.

MATERIALS

- bar magnet
- D-cell battery
- dc power supply
- large nail
- galvanometer
- metal paper clips
- small compasses
- wire
- wire coil with iron core

SAFETY

- Never close a circuit until it has been approved by your teacher. Never rewire or adjust any element of a closed circuit. Never work with electric current near water; be sure the floor and all work surfaces are dry.

- If the pointer on any kind of meter moves off scale, open the circuit immediately by opening the switch or disconnecting the power source.

- Do not attempt this exercise with any batteries, electrical devices, or magnets other than those provided by your teacher for this purpose.

- Wire coils may heat up rapidly during this experiment. If heating occurs, open the circuit immediately and handle the equipment with a hot mitt. Allow all equipment to cool before storing it.

MEET THE CHALLENGE

1. Before you begin, write a plan to demonstrate that an electric current can produce a magnetic field and that a changing magnetic field can produce an electric current. Determine what evidence you will be looking for, how you will measure or observe it, and how you will record your findings.

2. Familiarize yourself with the equipment provided; make sure you know how to use it safely and effectively. Make diagrams showing how you plan to use the equipment in your investigation.

3. Your teacher may add other requirements, such as submitting your plan for approval before conducting the investigation.

4. Address the items in the Documentation section on the next page.

TIPS

- Identify the requirements of the challenge, and make sure your plan addresses them fully.

- Review the materials and options. Is there one way to use the equipment to satisfy all the requirements, or will you need to perform different investigations using different apparatus setups?

- In your plan, identify the conditions you will test and how you will determine whether an electric current produces a magnetic field and whether a changing magnetic field produces a current.

- Consider whether the direction of the current or the speed or direction of the changing magnetic field affects the results.

DOCUMENTATION

1. What evidence did you find that an electric current produces a magnetic field?

2. **Evidence** Identify the evidence you found in your investigations, including the following:
   - evidence that an electric current produces a magnetic field
   - evidence that a changing magnetic field produces an electric current
   - a description of what happened when the direction of the current was reversed
   - a description of what happened when the direction or the speed of the moving magnetic field was changed

3. **Extend** Identify at least one practical application of the relationships you identified between electric currents and magnetic fields. Describe how you could use the equipment provided in the lab to create and test a model of your idea. If there is time and your teacher approves your plan, build your model and test your idea.

HS-PS3-1: Energy in a System

HS-PS3-1 Create a computational model to calculate the change in the energy of one component in a system when the change in energy of the other component(s) and energy flows in and out of the system are known.

Challenge Activity

Challenge: Create a mathematical model of a system that accounts for the movement of energy through a system.

In this activity, you will use your knowledge of work and the conservation of energy to model a system. First, using the ring stand, the pendulum clamp, the large hooked metal sphere, and the string, create a pendulum. The length of the pendulum should be 0.5 m. When the pendulum is swinging, the sphere should be as close to the table as possible without touching it. Set the small cardboard box so that the sphere strikes it right as the pendulum swings past its rest position (as the pendulum hangs at rest, it should just barely touch the cardboard box). Mark the cardboard box's initial position. Raise the pendulum's sphere so that the taut string makes a 15° angle from its rest position. Using this model, you will analyze the energy present in each part of the system during each of the following stages:

1. The pendulum is hanging in its rest position.

2. The pendulum's sphere is raised so that the taut string makes a 15° angle from its rest position.

3. The pendulum has swung down to its rest position, right before striking the box.

4. The pendulum has swung down to its rest position, right after striking the box.

5. The pendulum has hit the box and reached its highest point. The box has stopped moving.

MATERIALS

- balance
- large hooked metal sphere (about 200 g)
- masking tape
- meter sticks (at least two)
- pendulum clamp
- protractor
- ring stand
- small cardboard box
- string

SAFETY

Stay clear of the pendulum as it moves through its swing.

MEET THE CHALLENGE

1. Develop a series of equations to model the energy of the system. Use your knowledge of work and the conservation of energy as well as the mass of the sphere, m_s, and the mass of the box, m_b.

2. Set up the apparatus as described near the beginning of the Challenge Activity. Measure any variables necessary for calculating the energy in the system.

3. Perform the experiment by raising the pendulum so that the taut string makes a 15° angle from its rest position. Measure any variables necessary for calculating the energy in the system.

4. Release the pendulum and allow it to strike the box. Wait until the box has stopped moving. Measure any variables necessary for calculating the energy in the system.

TIPS

- Consider what you know about work and the conservation of energy as well as which variables of the system can be measured and which variables need to be solved for.

- Unless instructed not to, assume no energy is lost from the system in the collision between the sphere and the cardboard box.

- Pendulums lose very little energy each time they swing. It can be assumed that unless acted upon by an outside force, the pendulum maintains a constant level of mechanical energy.

- These equations may prove useful:

  - work done on an object: $W_{net} = F_{net}d \cos\theta$

  - kinetic energy of an object: $KE = \frac{1}{2}mv^2$

  - gravitational potential energy of an object: $PE_g = mgh$

HS-PS3-1: Energy in a System *continued*

DOCUMENTATION

1. Outline your series of equations for modeling the energy of the system. Explain the assumptions you made and the variables you used.

2. **Summarizing Data** Summarize your findings and observations, including an analysis of any data tables, charts, or graphs that you produced. Include the following:

   • the amount and type of energy present in each object during the five stages listed at the beginning of this Challenge Activity

   • the summary of your findings and observations

3. **Analysis** Consider how the energy moved through the system. How was energy introduced and lost from the system?

   • At which stages was energy introduced or lost from the system? At which stages did energy transfer between objects or transform between types of energy?

   • What work was done to introduce energy to the system? What work was done to remove energy from the system?

HS-PS3-2: Modeling Energy

HS-PS3-2 Develop and use models to illustrate that energy at the macroscopic scale can be accounted for as a combination of energy associated with the motions of particles (objects) and energy associated with the relative positions of particles (objects).

Challenge Activity

Challenge: Develop models that demonstrate energy at the macroscopic level as it relates to the kinetic energy of particles or objects as well as the potential energy associated with those particles or objects.

Energy is found everywhere in the study of physics, from the kinetic energy of gas molecules to the gravitational potential energy of a piano suspended by a crane high above a city sidewalk. In everyday situations, we usually think about energy when we see something moving or when we need to use energy to accomplish a task. Many of the types of energy we rely on are invisible to us, and they can be somewhat hard to understand, such as the potential energy of the rock formation shown below. Scientists often create models to help them understand phenomena and relationships that are difficult to study directly. Models can be drawings, comic strips, computer simulations, demonstrations, sculptures, or even choreographed human movement. The best models can even be used to predict what will happen under different conditions. In this Challenge Activity, you will develop a model or series of models to demonstrate how energy at the macroscopic level is related to the kinetic or potential energy of particles or objects. Consider all the types of energy you have studied as you create your model.

MATERIALS

modeling materials as needed or as provided by your teacher

HS-PS3-2: Modeling Energy *continued*

MEET THE CHALLENGE

1. Think of examples of energy-related phenomena you are familiar with, or those you've studied in class. Choose a situation that you'd like to model, and identify the relationships your model will demonstrate.

2. Based on the situation you've chosen, write a plan for what your model will show. Include the questions you have about the concepts as well as questions you think others might have. Decide what type of model will be best for the relationships you are planning to show. Examples of models could include diagrams, drawings, descriptions, and computer simulations. Decide what materials you will need.

3. Obtain your materials and set up any apparatus you will need. Take appropriate safety precautions. As you work on your model, test it to make sure it accurately represents the concepts and answers the questions you've identified. Include documentation, such as labels or scripts, that explains how your model works.

TIPS

- When developing models, think of concepts you find confusing or have questions about. The process of developing and using a model can help you understand the ideas better.

- Take some time to research other models that have been developed to study scientific concepts. What do successful models have in common? While some models can be quite elaborate, simple models can also be quite powerful. Remember that the value of a model in science is how it helps you understand a given phenomenon.

- As you develop your model, discuss it with others. Demonstrate your model to someone and find out what questions he or she has. Based on this feedback, consider modifying your model or adding documentation to address all questions. As a challenge, use your model to explain your ideas to someone who hasn't studied physics to see if it helps him or her understand an unfamiliar concept.

DOCUMENTATION

1. Complete your model and all the documentation required to demonstrate it or use it. Be prepared to demonstrate your model and explain how it works.

2. **Features** Prepare documentation to accompany your model. Identify the main features of your model and make sure you include explanations of how your model relates to energy. Your explanations should be clear and complete. They should provide enough information to answer questions or to allow someone to use your model to answer questions about the phenomenon.

3. **Analysis** Describe how well your model met the requirements of the challenge. What other models did you consider, and why did you decide against them? Were there any challenges or obstacles you faced that required you to change your plan? Identify ways in which your model is a good match for the phenomenon and ways in which it falls short. If you could, how would you improve your model?

HS-PS3-3: Energy of a Spring

HS-PS3-3 Design, build, and refine a device that works within given constraints to convert one form of energy into another form of energy.*

*denotes the integration of traditional science content with an engineering practice

Challenge Activity

Challenge: Design and develop, within constraints, a device that spring-launches a ball to reach a specified height.

A friend is putting on a puppet show and has asked you to help with a special effect. A scale-model soccer ball needs to be tossed briefly above a scale-model fence. The friend thinks that a device would be the most reliable way to get the ball to the correct height during each performance, rather than tossing the ball by hand.

You have a ball of the correct size and a file folder that shows the height of the fence. You also have a spring, similar to the one shown in the image below, to propel the ball upward. Other materials may be available.

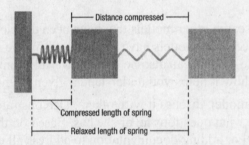

Develop a way to toss the ball straight up such that the bottom of the ball rises above the top of the fence. Ideally the ball should rise 0.5 cm above the fence, but heights as much as 3.0 cm above the fence will work without interfering with other pieces of scenery. Please ensure that the spring cannot propel any object that might be a danger.

MATERIALS
- assortment of springs
- cardboard, tape, string, markers, paper clips, scissors, or other materials (optional)
- file folder
- ruler (optional)
- safety goggles
- scale or balance (optional)
- small ball, 2–3 cm diameter

SAFETY

Wear goggles to perform this lab.

MEET THE CHALLENGE

1. Use at least one engineering design cycle to design, test, and revise a device to meet the challenge. You can use the tips provided as you wish. You may need to submit your design for review before building the first version or making major changes.

2. Develop supporting material describing your device, including an accurate visual of your final design and evidence that your design meets the challenge consistently.

3. Your teacher may require peer review of designs or request that you produce additional items, such as instructions for use.

4. Address the items listed in the Documentation section, and be prepared to demonstrate your design.

TIPS

- Identify and record the criteria and constraints of the challenge. Be sure to follow any design guidelines that your teacher may provide.

- Identify the system. Describe how the system changes from the time of the initial state to the time when the criteria are met.

- Is the system open or closed? Do you think the challenge is more about matter, more about energy, or about both equally? Consider your answer in terms of what is moving into, out of, and within the system.

- Review the materials and options provided for the challenge. What factors can you change easily to adjust the design of your device? What other factors, beyond the provided materials and options, might be possible to change? Are any of these changes likely to help you meet the challenge? After you've completed your first tests, try adjusting these factors individually to improve your results.

- Take notes and pay attention to safety. Determine how to use the controls in your system. If the spring should be compressed a certain distance, for example, design a way to achieve that distance reliably.

DOCUMENTATION

1. Provide evidence of how your design addresses the challenge. Include test results from your final design.

2. **Features** Identify the main features of your design and the purpose of each. Include the following:

   - important components of the system

   - source of energy

   - explanation of why the ball rises the correct amount reliably

3. **Tradeoffs** Identify any criteria or constraints that are not fully addressed by your design, along with any tradeoffs you made.

HS-PS3-4: Cooling Rates

HS-PS3-4 Plan and conduct an investigation to provide evidence that the transfer of thermal energy when two components of different temperature are combined within a closed system results in a more uniform energy distribution among the components in the system (second law of thermodynamics).

Challenge Activity

Challenge: Investigate two related problems and provide evidence to support your proposed solutions.

Practice To help you relate everyday experiences to the physics of heat and temperature, brief practice activities are recommended.

Problem A On a particular day, a coffee drinker must pour her coffee about ten minutes before she will be able to drink it. She knows the coffee will cool, but she wants it to remain as hot as possible. She will add room-temperature cream to the coffee. Is it better to add the cream, stir the coffee, and let it sit for ten minutes? Or is it better to let the coffee sit for ten minutes and then add and stir in the cream?

Problem B On a different day, the coffee drinker wishes to drink the coffee and cream right away, but it is too hot. She does not want to add anything else to the drink and is in a hurry. What are her best options to cool the coffee quickly?

MATERIALS

- containers with water at different temperatures
- measuring devices, such as thermometers or probeware
- materials or tools for heating and cooling materials, such as ice or a hot plate
- materials to heat and cool, such as water, metal, stone, heat-resistant plastic, or silicone
- material(s) to use as models for solving the problems, such as water
- scale or balance

SAFETY

- Ensure that the water is no hotter than 50°C (122°F) and that other materials to be touched are at safe temperatures. Plan to take appropriate cautions when working with hot plates and with hot and cold materials. Have your teacher approve your safety plan.

HS-PS3-4: Cooling Rates *continued*

MEET THE CHALLENGE

1. **Practice** Understand the experience and physics of temperature.

   a. Either work through the Section 9.1 QuickLab, Sensing Temperature, or design and carry out a different experiment in which you touch materials that are at different temperatures. If you have already worked through the lab, use your notes for Step 1b.

   b. For each part of the experiment, explain the transfer of energy and the change in temperature of your hand and of the water or other material.

   c. Find two materials that are both at room temperature but feel as if they are different temperatures when you touch them. Alternatively, recall a time when you have had this experience. Repeat Step 1b for this situation.

2. Determine your recommendations to the coffee drinker for Problems A and B provided in the Documentation section. Discuss the basis for your recommendations with others and come to a consensus.

TIPS

• You may wish to adapt the Section 9.1 QuickLab to use coffee cups or other small containers rather than basins. Consider the temperature of your skin as well as the temperature of the water.

• In Practice Steps 1b and 1c, you may wish to use a diagram, analogy, or model to explain each phenomenon. Check that you are accounting for all of the energy in the system.

• To meet the challenge, you may need to perform additional tests, do research online or in a library, and/or make calculations. To provide data to support your arguments, you may wish to perform or adapt the Section 9.2 Probeware Lab, Newton's Law of Cooling.

• Think about the systems involved in each of the coffee drinker's two problems, as you did in Steps 1b and 1c for the practice situations. Consider the temperatures and the changes of energy of different parts of the system in each problem.

• For Problem B, evaluate some of the actions people typically take to cool hot food. You might have additional ideas; there is no definitive answer.

DOCUMENTATION

1. Provide an analysis of energy transfer and temperature changes to explain why a substance at one temperature might feel either warm or cool and why two different substances at room temperature might feel as if they have two different temperatures.

2. **Problem A** The coffee drinker wants her coffee to be as hot as possible after ten minutes. Should she stir room-temperature cream into the hot coffee right away or just before drinking it? Provide evidence to justify your answer. State whether your recommendation represents the consensus of the class.

3. **Problem B** The coffee drinker wants to cool the coffee quickly. What do you recommend? Compare your choices with other alternatives and show why your recommendations are the best of the possibilities.

HS-PS3-5: Magnetic Field Interactions

HS-PS3-5 Develop and use a model of two objects interacting through electric or magnetic fields to illustrate the forces between objects and the changes in energy of the objects due to the interaction.

Challenge Activity

Challenge: Investigate magnetic fields and use observations to develop a model to illustrate the forces acting on objects and the resulting changes in energy.

Magnetic fields can be explored through the interactions of magnets with other magnets or with magnetic materials. A particularly interesting type of magnetic material is a ferrofluid—a liquid that becomes strongly magnetized when exposed to a magnetic field. In this activity, you will make a ferrofluid and use magnets and other magnetic materials to investigate magnetic field strength, forces, and energy. Based on your observations, you will develop a model to show the relationships among these properties.

MATERIALS

- 2-liter bottle preforms (or plastic petri dishes and resealable plastic bags)
- beaker
- fine metal filings (or magnetic laser printer toner) (15 mL)
- graduated cylinders
- magnets, assorted
- mineral oil (15 mL)
- paperclips (or other magnetic objects)
- ruler, nonmetallic
- stirring rod

SAFETY

- Wear safety goggles and an apron at all times.
- Wear a mask when measuring, transferring, and mixing iron filings.
- After handling filings or toner, make sure hands are clean before continuing the activity.

HS-PS3-5: Magnetic Field Interactions *continued*

MEET THE CHALLENGE

1. Start by mixing 15 mL of filings or toner with 15 mL of mineral oil. Always add the oil to the filings, never the other way around. Stir gently until thoroughly mixed. Hold a magnet to the side of the beaker and observe what happens. If spikes of ferrofluid form, the mixture is ready to use. If not, measure and add more filings/toner or oil until spikes form when a magnet is held to the side of the beaker. Make sure to measure and record the amounts and to mix well after every addition.

2. When your ferrofluid is ready, pour it into the bottle preform or petri dish and close the container. If using a petri dish, seal the dish inside a resealable plastic bag to prevent spills or leaks.

3. Use the magnets, compass, and other materials to explore what happens to magnetic materials in a magnetic field. How can you detect or measure the effects of a magnetic field? Make observations to determine what variables affect the amount of force on objects in the field.

4. Make drawings and take notes of your observations to use as you develop your model. Your model can be a drawing, a diagram, or a written explanation showing what happens when objects interact in a magnetic field.

TIP

As you complete the activity, make predictions about what you think will happen, and then test your predictions. If something happens that surprises you or doesn't match your predictions, repeat that trial to verify your results. Then conduct further investigations to explore further and clarify your understanding until you are able to predict the outcomes.

DOCUMENTATION

1. Complete your model and all the documentation required to explain what it shows.

2. **Features** Identify the main features of your model, and make sure you explain how your model relates to your observations. Your explanations should be clear and complete and should provide enough information to answer questions or to allow someone to use your model to answer questions about what happens to objects in a magnetic field.

3. **Analysis** Describe how well your model met the requirements of the challenge. Identify ways in which your model is a good match for the phenomenon and ways in which it falls short. If you could, how would you improve your model?

Waves and Their Applications in Technologies for Information Transfer

HS-PS4-1: Properties of Waves

HS-PS4-1 Use mathematical representations to support a claim regarding relationships among the frequency, wavelength, and speed of waves traveling in various media.

Challenge Activity

Challenge: Explore the properties of waves traveling in different media and use mathematical representations to describe what is observed.

In this activity, you will gather data and observations from a variety of different wave interactions, including waves traveling through different media, such as the ripple waves traveling through water in the image below. Based on the information collected, you will identify patterns and make a claim that describes the relationships among the frequency, wavelength, and speed of waves. Finally, you will describe the relationships using mathematical expressions, and show how the mathematical expressions support your claim.

MEET THE CHALLENGE

1. Your teacher will provide data, demonstrations, or materials for you to use as a source of information.

2. As you observe the behavior of waves in different media, make careful observations of the frequency, wavelength, and speed of the waves. For each type of wave, determine what observations or measurements to make and how to verify that your observations are accurate. Make sure you label your observations and record your data in an organized way so you can analyze it later.

3. Are you able to make quantitative measurements of every type of wave? If not, which properties can you measure, and which must you simply observe carefully? What are the factors that make some measurements difficult or impossible? Can you measure all the properties independently, or do you need to measure other quantities, such as time, and make calculations? For waves that are not visible, such as sound waves, how can you determine the frequency, wavelength, or speed of the wave? How confident are you in these measurements?

MEET THE CHALLENGE *continued*

4. Analyze your measurements and observations and look for patterns in the relationships among frequency, wavelength, and speed. How does the type of wave affect the relationships? How does the medium the wave is traveling through affect the relationships? Write a claim that describes a pattern you have identified in the relationships among these properties. How can you represent this pattern mathematically? Once you have come up with a mathematical representation, describe how the mathematical expressions support your claim about the relationships among frequency, wavelength, and speed of waves in different media.

5. Do your mathematical expressions apply to all the waves you studied? If not, explain why. If your observations and measurements are accurate, how can you adjust your mathematical representation to account for the difference?

TIPS

- Take organized notes. Repeat measurements and observations to verify your technique and reduce errors.

- Using standard notation for the variables in your mathematical representations will make it easier for you to compare your results to the equations in the book and to discuss your findings with your classmates. For example, use T for period, f for frequency, v for wave speed, and λ (the Greek letter lambda) for wavelength.

- Diagrams can be used to help show the relationship between mathematical representations and written descriptions. If you use diagrams, make sure they are clearly labeled and easy to understand.

DOCUMENTATION

1. Present your findings in an organized way that meets the criteria established by your teacher. Make sure your claim is clearly stated, and provide examples to show how your mathematical representation supports your claim.

2. **Features** What challenges did you encounter when you compared different types of waves? If waves were impossible to measure, explain why and describe how you made reliable observations of the properties. How did different media affect the waves you observed, and how did you account for that mathematically?

3. **Analysis** Which do you think is more accurate, your written claim or the mathematical representation? Which do you think is a better way to communicate your findings? Explain.

Waves and Their Applications in Technologies for Information Transfer

HS-PS4-2: Digital Versus Analog Signals

HS-PS4-2 Evaluate questions about the advantages of using a digital transmission and storage of information.

Challenge Activity

Challenge: Investigate the differences in reliability between analog and digital signals.

In this activity, you will investigate why digital signals have become the primary way that information is transmitted and stored. Since the advent of the home computer, more and more information has been transmitted in digital form. Even media historically transmitted as analog signals such as satellite television and radio have started to use digital encoding. Remember:

- An *analog signal* is a signal whose properties, such as amplitude and frequency, can change continuously in a given range.

- A *digital signal* is a signal that can be represented as a sequence of discrete values.

Analog signals transmit information in the form of a wave. Digital signals also send information in the form of a wave, but with a crucial difference, as illustrated in the image below. A digital wave rapidly switches between two values instead of constantly varying across a range of values. Analog signals send raw information that is then recorded or replicated as closely as possible by the receiver, while digital signals send a code that is decoded by the receiver into information.

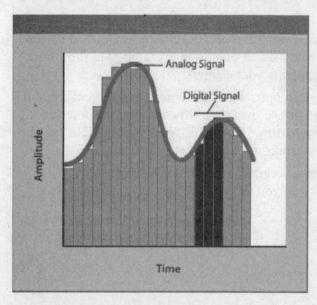

Though analog and digital signals are most often used in transmitting information via electromagnetic waves or current, such as using wireless networks, radios, or electrical wires, you will use sound to explore the differences between analog and digital signals:

- **Analog Signal Transmission:** You will explore how noise is introduced into the transmission of analog signals and consider the advantages and disadvantages of using these types of signals to transfer information.

- **Digital Signal Transmission:** You will explore how noise is introduced in the transmission of digital signals and compare the results to your experiences with analog signals transmission. Digital signals are waves that vary quickly between two values to produce a code that consists of 0s and 1s. This two-value code can be read by a computer and decoded into useful information. To model this, you will silence to model 0s and a loud sound to model 1s.

| HS-PS4-2: Digital Versus Analog Signals *continued*

MATERIALS

recording and playback devices (such as tape recorder and smartphone) (2)

MEET THE CHALLENGE

Analog Signal Transmission

1. Take one of the recording devices and record a ten second message.

2. Play back the recording from the original device while using the second device to record the playback. Listen to your new recording and note any differences between the recordings on the two devices.

3. Repeat this process until you have rerecorded your message ten times. Compare your final recording to the initial recording and note any differences.

Digital Signal Transmission

1. Take one of the recording devices and make a ten second recording. In your recording you will produce a rhythm. Sharply tapping a pen next to or on the microphone of the recording device produces a clear, loud sound.

2. Play back the recording from the original device while using the other device to record the playback from the first device. Listen to your new recording and note any differences between the recordings on the two devices.

3. Repeat this process until you have rerecorded your series of taps ten times. Compare your final recording to the initial recording and note any differences.

TIPS

- When rerecording your message from one device to another, keep the microphone of the device recording near the speakers of the device playing the message for optimal results.

- To experiment with the efficiency of the data transfer, you can vary the distance between the microphone and speakers of the two devices.

DOCUMENTATION

1. Describe how the activity models analog and digital signals.

2. **Summarizing Data** Summarize your findings and observations. Include:

   - the data that you collected during your experiment

   - the factors that seemed to affect the clarity of your recordings

   - the summary of your findings and observations

3. **Conclusions** Consider how your models of analog and digital signals behaved after several rerecordings:

   - Were either the analog or digital signals clearer after the signal had been rerecorded several times? What does this say about the reliability of transferring the two types of signals?

   - How was the recording affected by the distance between the microphone and speakers? What is an example of a signal transfer situation in the real world that behaves similarly depending on the distance between the transmitter and receiver?

Waves and Their Applications in Technologies for Information Transfer

HS-PS4-3: Wave and Particle Models

HS-PS4-3 Evaluate the claims, evidence, and reasoning behind the idea that electromagnetic radiation can be described either by a wave model or a particle model, and that for some situations one model is more useful than the other.

Challenge Activity

Challenge: Construct a guide, such as a comparison table or decision tree, to assist in decisions about which model to use for a given instance of electromagnetic radiation.

Electromagnetic radiation can be described using either a wave model or a particle model, but how do you decide which to use in a given situation? Collect information about the two models and examples of how each model is used. Evaluate the examples to determine the reasons for the choice of model. Then, construct a comparison table or other guide to help you make decisions about which model to use to describe situations involving electromagnetic radiation. Compare your model with those of other students and look for ways to improve it.

MATERIALS

- computer with Internet access
- note-taking/recording medium (for example, paper and pencil or a notetaking app)
- sources for document research (for example, library, Internet, or people)

MEET THE CHALLENGE

1. List the variables and equations most used for waves. Do all apply to electromagnetic radiation?

2. List the important variables and equations most used for the interactions of particles, such as equations that describe collisions. Do all apply to electromagnetic radiation?

3. List the shared variables and conversion factors, such as the energy of a photon in terms of frequency.

4. Choose a variety of items from the list of examples provided. For each item, determine whether both models are equally useful or whether one is best. It may be helpful to consider the reason(s) each model does or does not work well. Do you find any patterns in the choice of model? Try to generalize your results.

5. Find a few more examples that involve electromagnetic radiation and repeat step 4.

6. Make a guide to help you quickly determine which model to use in a given situation. You might make a table of when to use the wave model, the particle model, or either. You might instead use a decision chart, a concept map, or other way of organizing the information you need.

7. With a classmate or in a small group, compare your guides. Look for ways to add to your guide or other ways to improve it. Implement any reasonable changes.

EXAMPLES

- Light shining through a small hole produces a diffraction pattern.
- An antenna receives a radio signal and supplies a matching analog current to a speaker.
- A warm object gives off a spectrum of radiation that depends only on its temperature.
- An accelerating charge produces electromagnetic radiation.
- A photoelectric detector produces a current only when light above a certain frequency shines on it.
- Sunlight bounces off ocean waves. Some of the light reaches your eye.
- A converging lens produces a real image.
- A ray optics diagram shows how a convex mirror produces a virtual image.
- Water droplets in the air produce a rainbow in sunlight.
- A glow stick gives off light when two fluids mix.
- A view of a neon light through a spectroscope shows a series of lines of red and other colors.
- Ultraviolet light breaks down ozone in the upper atmosphere.
- Ultraviolet light is used to sterilize surgical instruments.
- X-rays pass through muscle but are absorbed by bone, producing an image on a photographic plate.
- Gamma rays are usually characterized by their energy rather than by their wavelength.

DOCUMENTATION

1. Produce your guide. Make it neat and clear enough to be graded.

2. Demonstrate your guide by evaluating the models for one or more new examples from your teacher or classmates. Give reasons that each model is a good or a poor choice for the particular example.

Waves and Their Applications in Technologies for Information Transfer

HS-PS4-4: Claims Concerning Electromagnetic Radiation

HS-PS4-4 Evaluate the validity and reliability of claims in published materials of the effects that different frequencies of electromagnetic radiation have when absorbed by matter.

Challenge Activity

Challenge: Apply information gained in class and from the *Student Edition* to evaluate published claims regarding the effects of electromagnetic radiation.

Electromagnetic radiation is a form of energy. When absorbed by matter, it can have a range of effects, from warming solid substances to ionizing atoms. These effects depend on the frequency and sometimes on the amount of the radiation. Ionizing radiation, for example, is used in solar cells to produce electric current, but it can also be destructive to materials, including living tissue. It is well known that prolonged exposure to ultraviolet radiation from the sun can lead to painful burns and even skin cancer.

Sunlight, however, is only one source of electromagnetic radiation. Today's world is awash in electromagnetic radiation from numerous sources, including cell phones, wireless networks, global positioning system devices, and television and radio broadcasts. Might this radiation also be affecting our bodies, our foods, or other organisms and materials around us?

Find published sources that address an issue related to the effects of electromagnetic radiation on matter. List your sources in a table like the one provided, and then consider the questions that follow as you evaluate your sources and form an opinion about the validity and reliability of the claims that are made in the source.

MATERIALS

- computer with Internet access
- other news and information sources (for example, television newscasts, documentaries, expert interviews, and product information sheets)
- school or public library

HS-PS4-4: Claims Concerning Electromagnetic Radiation *continued*

MEET THE CHALLENGE

1. Use a table to organize your sources.

Source Title	Author(s)	Publication Year	Reliability (1 to 5)

2. Analyze your sources and information with the help of the Questions provided.

3. Organize your research and prepare a presentation as described in the Documentation section.

QUESTIONS

• What criteria did you use to evaluate your sources? If a source contains data, how reliable do you think the data set is? Why?

• How does electromagnetic radiation affect matter? Should all electromagnetic radiation be considered potentially harmful because some forms are harmful? How might you draw distinctions between the harmful forms and the nonharmful forms?

• After consulting all your sources, describe other experiments or studies that you think should be conducted that might help explain the effects that different frequencies of electromagnetic radiation have when absorbed by matter. Do you feel a proven cause-and-effect relationship can be established?

• Are there any aspects of your sources that you think are questionable? Do you feel your sources can all be equally trusted? What are some reasons why an author or a group might wish to emphasize the effects of electromagnetic radiation on matter? Why might other authors or groups wish to downplay them?

DOCUMENTATION

Prepare a poster, a report, or another type of presentation describing the effects that different frequencies of electromagnetic radiation have when absorbed by matter. Use your sources, as well as information from the *Student Edition*, to support your claims. As your teacher permits, the presentation can be completed on your own or in collaboration with others. If you can find a partner who has discovered other sources and formed an opinion that varies from your own, examine the differences among the sources and debate why your ideas might be different. In discussing your points, try to understand why some individuals or groups might hold a different opinion, and directly address their concerns.

Waves and Their Applications in Technologies for Information Transfer

HS-PS4-5: Technological Applications of Waves

HS-PS4-5 Communicate technical information about how some technological devices use the principles of wave behavior and wave interactions with matter to transmit and capture information and energy.*

*denotes the integration of traditional science content with an engineering practice

Challenge Activity

Challenge: Research a technological device that relies on wave behavior and interactions. Create a technical manual describing how the device functions.

Devices you use every day rely on the manipulation of wave behaviors and interactions. From radio broadcasts to cell phones to x-ray machines, waves are transmitting information and energy.

In this Challenge Activity, you will select a technological device that is important or interesting to you. Research the details of how this device uses wave behavior and wave interactions to function. Organize the information into a technical manual that describes the parts of this device and explain how this device uses waves to manage information and/or energy.

MATERIALS

• computer with Internet access
• note-taking/recording medium (for example, paper and pencil or a notetaking app)
• school or public library
• *Student Edition*

MEET THE CHALLENGE

1. Review the *Student Edition* to find introductory examples of technological devices that rely on wave behaviors and wave interactions. Some examples appear in Section 14.3, Optical Phenomena; Section 15.3, Lasers; and Section 20.4, Electromagnetic Waves.

2. Consider technological devices that are interesting or important to you. Do any of those devices rely on wave behaviors and interactions?

3. Select a device that you would like to understand in greater detail. Confirm with your teacher or through preliminary research that your chosen device uses waves to transmit or store energy and information.

4. Perform detailed research to understand the components and function of your device, including the particular characteristics and behaviors of waves that the device employs.

5. Complete the tasks outlined in the Documentation section.

TIPS

• Check with your teacher before planning to provide a demonstration of your technological device.

• Cite the sources you use in your research. Ask your teacher if you need help finding reliable research material.

DOCUMENTATION

1. Produce a technical manual describing the function of your technological device. The manual should include the following:

   • a description of the device's components

   • diagrams showing the how the device works and how the components are involved

   • diagrams and descriptions detailing the wave behaviors or interactions are used by the device

2. Think about the device you described in your technical manual.

   • Provide an example of a device that is likely to use waves in a similar manner.

   • Provide an example of a device that is likely to use waves in a different manner.

Engineering Design

HS-ETS1-1: Criteria and Constraints

HS-ETS1-1 Analyze a major global challenge to specify qualitative and quantitative criteria and constraints for solutions that account for societal needs and wants.

Challenge Activity

Challenge: Make a guide to help someone think through the aspects of a decision about energy resources.

Energy resources—such as fossil fuels, solar energy, and nuclear energy—have associated costs, benefits, and risks. Costs include the amount of money paid, but also include something that is given up, lost, or damaged. During the Industrial Revolution (1760–1840), energy resources were used with only limited consideration of this second type of cost—resulting in pollution, the emission of greenhouse gases, and the depletion of nonrenewable resources. Today, there are international agreements that limit some uses to avoid these costs. However, the restrictions can make it more difficult for developing countries to become industrialized and to benefit from the resulting growth.

When an individual, community, country, or international group makes a decision about energy resources, others are affected. Some of the consequences might not be obvious, such as the costs or benefits that occur before the decision maker uses the energy. For example, the waste products of a power plant may not be obvious to someone using electrical power.

Explore a decision related to energy resources that a person or group might need to make, such as developing high-speed rail service using maglev or other technology. Identify the types of criteria and constraints that the decision maker should take into consideration. Then make a guide to help someone consider the criteria and constraints specific to their decision.

MEET THE CHALLENGE

1. Choose a topic that interests you and involves energy resources. Also choose an audience—that is, the decision maker who will use the guide you make. Your focus might be very limited, such as an individual choosing a small appliance or deciding how to cook food on a hot day. At the other extreme, you might address a global issue, such as an environmental decision that must be made by a group of international lawmakers.

2. Identify the main factors to consider in a decision involving energy resources. It may be helpful to exchange information with other students during this step. You may want to look up examples of energy resources and energy usage to ensure that you have identified most of the major issues. Don't limit your list to scientific issues. Include social, personal, aesthetic, and other issues. These issues may be important factors in a decision even if they can't be evaluated scientifically.

3. Recast your thoughts into criteria, constraints, and tradeoffs as a way to help guide decisions. Include lists, tables, flowcharts, or other means to help the decision maker gather information, review criteria and constraints, and evaluate the tradeoffs for a particular situation.

4. When you have a draft of your guide, exchange guides with other students and give peer reviews. Give feedback on the issues in the guide and also on its ease of use.

5. Improve your guide before submitting it to your teacher. Use your teacher's comments to improve your guide further if you wish to publish it.

DOCUMENTATION

1. Submit your guide. Be sure to identify the purpose and audience for your guide. Your teacher may ask for a copy of your guide in a format suited for adding comments.

2. Cite your sources and any resources that you recommend for the decision maker.

3. Explain how your guide is connected to global issues.

   • Note the ways in which your guide touches on the big issues related to energy resources.

   • Characterize the general human or societal need(s) that your guide reflects.

   • Consider how your guide might be related to other global issues, and then describe any strong relationships you find.

Your teacher might specify the form for this information. If the choice is left to you, consider including it in an oral presentation of your guide to the class, producing it as a separate document, or integrating it into your guide. For example, you might help motivate a decision maker to reduce his or her ecological footprint or to minimize the release of greenhouse gases.

| HS-ETS1-1: Criteria and Constraints *continued*

TIPS

You may wish to do Challenge steps 1 and 2 together. Understanding general issues related to energy resources may help you choose a topic.

Step 2 Suggestions

- You might start by listing general types of costs, benefits, and risks. For example, a school's costs for overhead lighting might include the initial installation, the replacement of bulbs, and the ongoing power consumption. The choice of lights might affect the school's reputation for environmental responsibility ("being green") or the resulting attractiveness of the space.

- You might think of pros and cons or of ways someone might oppose or support a particular choice. For example, pros and cons for different choices of overhead lighting might include the brightness and the color of the light, how hot the fixture gets, frequency of bulb replacement, and how well the light meets the lighting needs.

- You might imagine the qualities of a successful solution or consider intended and unintended consequences. Use any way of thinking that works for you. You might try several ways of thinking and/or several sources of information. Your results can be messy at this stage because you will organize them in step 3.

Limit the Problem

If your topic is complex, keep your guide manageable by choosing just the top few issues that will affect the decision. You may also wish to put the most effort into the issues most closely related to the science you have been learning.

Criteria, Constraints, and Tradeoffs

- To identify criteria for an energy situation, record the needs and wants—the purposes filled by the use of energy resources.

- To identify constraints, record the limitations, such as a maximum budget or the desire to avoid the risk of harm.

- Look at the criteria and constraints together. Are any likely to be in conflict? Identify the tradeoffs that the decision maker should consider. Think about the form to use for this important part of your guide. Walk through a sample decision in your mind and think about whether lists, tables, flowcharts, or other devices would be helpful.

Ranking and Rating

- The decision maker might find it useful to rank items by importance. Recommend ranking items if you think it might be helpful

- As an alternative to ranking items, the decision maker might rate them, perhaps by classifying each as low, medium, or high priority. If applicable, try to formulate or find a rating scale that can be used to make comparisons for this particular set of criteria or constraints. Recommend rating items if you think it might be helpful.

| HS-ETS1-1: Criteria and Constraints *continued*

Quantitative Measures and Sample Values

- It may be helpful for the decision maker to look at numerical values, such as available funds or cubic meters of a gas pollutant. He or she might consider relative values, such as the balance between price and income. In your guide, include ways for the decision maker to record and use these values. If you think it would be helpful, provide sample values, such as the current typical prices of two energy sources.

- Look at the sample values you might provide. Can you use them to save the decision maker the time of looking up actual values? For example, if the local costs of cooking with two energy sources are nearly the same, then the decision maker might use your sample values to decide to focus on a different issue. If the costs are very different, your sample values might allow the decision maker to make good-enough estimates rather than look up actual costs.

Priorities

Help the decision maker be efficient. Perhaps the options for one tradeoff are likely to be close and difficult to evaluate. If a different tradeoff would be easier to evaluate and would produce a decision more quickly, then present this tradeoff first.

Format and Labels

- Choose a format for your guide that best suits the audience and your available technology. For example, if you wish to hand-draw a decision flowchart, or if your guide should be kept in a certain location, then you might design a physical booklet or pamphlet. If your recommendations include gathering information from online, your guide might be in the form of a webpage or other digital resource.

- Use clear labels to help ensure that the purpose of your guide will be clear to the intended audience.

Test and Iterate

Imagine making the decision yourself and test the usefulness of your guide. Look for areas you can improve. Consider leaving out material that is less important.

HS-ETS1-2: Design a Lighting Plan

HS-ETS1-2 Design a solution to a complex real-world problem by breaking it down into smaller, more manageable problems that can be solved through engineering.

Challenge Activity

Challenge: Recommend a lighting plan for a school or a classroom.

Many schools rely on fluorescent tube lights, which are generally more efficient to run than incandescent lights. In the years since many schools were built, different forms of fluorescent lights, such as compact fluorescents (CFs), have become affordable. The lighting industry also has developed and continues to improve practical light-emitting diode (LED) bulbs. These lights use less energy to produce the same amount of light as incandescent lights. LED bulbs typically cost more but last longer. Sometimes new fixtures are required to accommodate new types of bulbs.

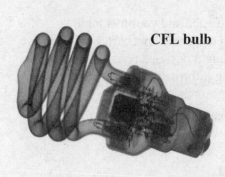
CFL bulb

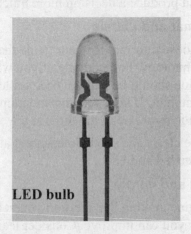
LED bulb

    Recommend a lighting plan for your school or classroom. The ideal recommendation is environmentally responsible and saves money in the short, medium, and long terms.

MEET THE CHALLENGE

1. Decide how to break down the problem into smaller pieces. You might evaluate the school or classroom's current lighting, decide on the most important changes, and then make recommendations of how and when to make those changes. Or you might start with an ideal lighting plan and look for ways to bring the existing system closer to the ideal. Think about these and other approaches, and then make a choice.

2. Plan your approach. What will you need for each step? What will you do? If a step depends on the results of previous steps, make contingency plans.

3. Your teacher will set expectations for this challenge. If you wish to exceed the expectations, such as by comparison shopping or by doing an experiment, then submit that part of your plan to your teacher for approval.

4. Implement your plan. Make adjustments as you go.

5. Gather your results and use them to make a recommendation.

DOCUMENTATION

1. Produce a summary of your recommendations. Put it in a form that would help someone implement your plan, such as a checklist or a diagram. If you recommend making the changes over time, then indicate this aspect in your summary, such as by labeling Phase 1 and Phase 2 changes.

2. Provide a separate document with supporting details. Including the information and the sources you used. Explain the tradeoffs, and explain the reasoning for your choices. If any tradeoffs depend on future conditions, such as prices during a later phase, suggest a way to make the decision at the appropriate time. If any choices depend on personal preferences, provide a recommendation and also explain how the school officials could adjust your plan to suit different preferences.

TIPS

- You may find it useful to identify criteria and constraints for the desired lighting plan. These factors might include social or aesthetic considerations as well as financial costs and scientific factors. You might also wish to identify priorities, such as correcting problems, improving efficiency, or increasing environmental friendliness.

- If the time allowed for the challenge is limited, you may want to focus on just a few parts of the problem, such as improving the light in specific areas and reducing energy use. Other aspects of the lighting system can be left unchanged (rather than optimized).

- If you do this challenge as a full investigation, start by doing research. Guides to architectural design, interior design, home improvement, and commercial products can be good places to start. You might get a more complete picture if you consult several different types of sources.

- Photographs and other visuals may help you remember, describe, and communicate information about lighting. (Cite your sources.)

- Think about the purposes of the existing lights. Ambient lights provide general illumination. Task lights give more light for a particular purpose or in a particular area. Accent lights produce visual interest. You might identify other functions, such as safety lights, emergency lights, and warming lamps. These purposes result in different desirable characteristics.

- For task lighting, shadows and glare can be important factors. The placement and angle of the light can affect how functional it is. Sometimes diffusing the light or adding a second source can solve a problem.

- Too much light can sometimes cause more problems than too little light. (If you are familiar with the inverse-square law, you may be able to estimate when a small change in position is likely to have a big effect on outcome.)

- Decisions about the replacement of equipment often involve tradeoffs between the cost of the change and the savings in ongoing costs, such as energy use and bulb replacement. To make comparisons, it can be useful to calculate the time it would take for these two factors to be equal. The result is sometimes called the break-even point.

HS-ETS1-2: Design a Lighting Plan *continued*

Lighting Systems

- There are several ways to use the idea of a system to help you devise a lighting plan. You might consider how the parts interact. You might think of input, output, controls, and feedback in terms of the light or in terms of the energy used.

- Think about how sunlight contributes to the lighting system. The direction and amount of sunlight change during the day and over the year.

- Windows, skylights, and the absence or presence of walls and other surfaces are ways of directing, reflecting, and diffusing light.

- Surfaces that reflect and diffuse light can change the effectiveness of lights. As a short test, watch as someone opens and closes a book in bright light. Observe how the light on the person changes as the book's pages reflect more light.

- Lights may interact with other systems. For example, lights may dim when certain equipment is in use, or lights may affect the temperature in an area.

Engineering Design

HS-ETS1-3: Tradeoffs

HS-ETS1-3 Evaluate a solution to a complex real-world problem based on prioritized criteria and trade-offs that account for a range of constraints, including cost, safety, reliability, and aesthetics, as well as possible social, cultural, and environmental impacts.

Challenge Activity

Challenge: Evaluate the use of an alternative energy source based on a set of criteria.

The sources of energy used in communities each have a combination of pros and cons. It is easy to compare two prices, but it is harder to compare different qualities, such as the relative values of human risk and environmental impact.

For this challenge, imagine that your team has been hired to advise a community council that is considering a proposal for the use of an alternative energy source, such as the one pictured below. The community's energy demands have been increasing. Members of the council have listed a variety of issues and negotiated some priorities. Your job is to evaluate the proposed energy source according to the list and then report your findings to the council.

MEET THE CHALLENGE

Part 1: Set up the details of the challenge.

1. Your teacher will identify the community and the alternative energy source. Review the list of criteria and constraints and make the following adjustments:

   • Adjust the criteria and constraints to fit the community and the energy source.

   • You may divide items on the list into separate criteria and/or constraints.

   • You may propose adding or removing items, but ensure that the list represents the range of factors in HS-ETS1-3.

   • If the community is fictional, you may need to invent reasonable characteristics to fill in important details. For example, you may need to determine whether the new energy source needs to be reliable mostly for peak usage periods, at all ordinary times, or even in emergency conditions.

2. Choose a rating scale, such as 0 (not relevant) to 5 (very important). Roll a number cube or use another means to assign random values to each of the criteria and constraints below. You may then switch any two values to make the results more reasonable. You may make up to two additional switches.

3. Your teacher will tell you what type of report the council wants.

Part 2: Evaluate the proposed energy source and advise the council.

4. Identify the tradeoffs and evaluate the use of the energy source in the community.

5. Prepare and deliver your report for the council.

DOCUMENTATION

Your report for the council should meet the challenge in the format specified.

Criteria and Constraints

- The community needs more energy to meet increased demands reliably.

- The council's decision should be compatible with the values of the community.

- The decision should benefit members of the community equally.

- Nobody's safety should be put at risk.

- Risks to property, pets, plants, livestock, crops, and the environment should be minimized.

- The initial price should be reasonable.

- The ongoing price of the energy should be as low as possible.

- The service and maintenance costs should be as low as possible. (Assume a 30-year timeline.)

- Installation should be easy to achieve (such as by hiring a contractor).

- Installation should cause minimal disruption or destruction.

- Any structures needed for the storage or use of the energy should not have a negative impact on the community (by blocking traffic, spoiling views, lowering property values, etc.).

- The costs and risks should be fairly distributed among community members.

- Use of the energy should be easy.

- Use of the energy should not cause disruption—such as noise or odors—or destruction.

- Waste should be minimized.

- The decision should be environmentally responsible ("green").

TIPS

- Switch values in step 2 to make the results more reasonable. Consider whether the community is likely to consider some issues to be the most important, such as money, other costs, fairness, or responsibility. Be aware that council members often represent a range of viewpoints, some of which may conflict.

- State tradeoffs in useful ways. For example, a tradeoff between getting the highest possible quality and spending the least money can be expressed as "getting the best value for the money."

- If your evaluation shows that the proposed energy source would be a good solution, or shows that it would be a bad solution, say so in your report. Otherwise, identify the most important tradeoffs for the council to consider.

- Before delivering your report, try to see it as a council member would. Would you be satisfied with it?

- Consider working with other groups to critique each other's reports so that you can improve them before finalizing them.

HS-ETS1-4: Model the Impact

HS-ETS1-4 Use a computer simulation to model the impact of proposed solutions to a complex real-world problem with numerous criteria and constraints on interactions within and between systems relevant to the problem.

Challenge Activity

Challenge: Explore one part of the complex issues of energy use and climate change by using a model to test proposed solutions.

The use of energy resources has complex effects on Earth's interacting spheres. For example, the extraction and burning of fossil fuels moves carbon from the geosphere to the atmosphere, typically in the form of carbon dioxide (CO_2). The production and use of biomass fuels moves carbon from the atmosphere to the biosphere and back again, although the system may also involve the use of other energy resources.

In the atmosphere, CO_2 acts as a greenhouse gas, absorbing and emitting radiation in a way that tends to keep energy in the Earth system, as shown in the graphic below. The resulting higher temperatures have many effects, such as causing ice to melt. Ice usually reflects sunlight more effectively than the ground or water do, so less ice means that more sunlight is absorbed into the Earth system. However, higher temperatures also cause more liquid water to evaporate, which can result in more clouds. Clouds reflect sunlight, so they prevent some solar energy from being absorbed by the Earth system. Clouds also reflect radiation from the ground, so they keep energy in the Earth system. Water vapor also acts as a greenhouse gas.

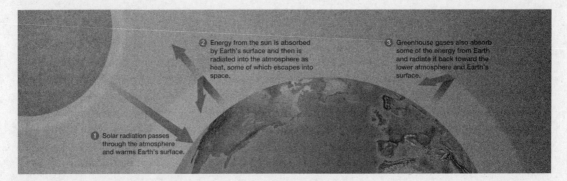

These feedback mechanisms are so complex that scientists can't make exact calculations for real-world situations. Instead, they make models with different simplifications and combine the effects of several models to make predictions. They might use one model to predict a change in temperature and a different model to explore how that change in temperature will affect sea level and coastlines. These models are often in the form of computer simulations.

In this Challenge Activity, you will use a computer simulation to model one aspect of a proposed solution for the use of energy resources. You will need to decide how to simplify the situation in order to use the model.

HS-ETS1-4: Model the Impact *continued*

MATERIALS

- computer with an Internet connection
- note-taking and data-analysis tools, such as a spreadsheet or a physical notebook and graph paper

SAFETY

Use safe Internet practices. If you conduct an Internet search for a model, do not download or open files from unknown sources. Protect your personal information.

MEET THE CHALLENGE

You may wish to do steps 1 and 2 together so that your alternatives and your model are well matched.

1. Choose the computer model that you will use to explore an impact of energy use. Most of the tips below are written for a specific model, "The Greenhouse Effect." If you wish to use a different model, identify the model and what you will do differently, and then have your teacher review your plan.

2. Choose at least two alternative solutions involving energy resources that you can model. For this challenge, you may use unrealistic scenarios, such as changing all energy use to a specific type, or using half of one type and half of another. Use the current situation, or a simplification of it, for comparison with the two alternatives.

3. Translate each alternative in step 2 into a set of inputs for the computer model. You will need to make some assumptions or other simplifications (see the tips on the next page). Test each set of inputs and record the results.

4. Use the model results to draw inferences about the solution(s).

DOCUMENTATION

1. Document your alternatives, your model, and the reasons for your choices.

2. Explain how the model inputs represent the alternatives. Identify the main simplifications that you made.

3. Present the model inputs and outputs (results) in an appropriate form. Make sure your audience can tell what's changing in the inputs and in the results.

4. Interpret the results and draw inferences. (You may wish to combine this information with #2 or with #3, if either makes sense for your work.)

5. You used a model to explore one part of a complex issue. Put your work in context by describing how the part you modeled relates to the issue as a whole.

HS-ETS1-4: Model the Impact *continued*

TIPS

These tips assume the use of the computer simulation, "The Greenhouse Effect" (see below for details). If you use a different model, adapt the tips to your chosen model and your matching set of solutions.

Using "The Greenhouse Effect"

• Use a search engine to search for "PhET" and "Greenhouse Effect"—you'll need to find and run the simulation from the University of Colorado. Select Download or Run Now according to your teacher's directions. Within the simulation, use the "Greenhouse Effect" tab at the top.

Choosing and Analyzing Solutions

• Think about the current situation, in which much of the world's energy use comes from fossil fuels. As people use fossil fuels, CO_2 is added to the atmosphere. You might model just this part of the system by ignoring other greenhouse gases and by assuming that the amount of CO_2 will increase by a certain amount each year. (If you wish, use different simplifications.) Decide how to adjust the inputs of your model in order to simulate the current situation. Try it. Make adjustments as needed. Then record the set of inputs you plan to use to model the current situation.

• Decide whether to include cloud formation. For example, you might choose a temperature at which you'll add a cloud (increased evaporation would put water into the atmosphere). If the temperature in any of your tests drops below this temperature, you would remove the cloud (precipitation would remove water from the atmosphere). You can use this procedure, develop and use a different procedure, or ignore clouds.

• Think about a different energy resource. Does it produce greenhouse gases? Does it release them or water vapor into the atmosphere? If people used that energy resource instead of fossil fuels, would it change the rate at which material is added to the atmosphere (increase/decrease per year)? How would the total amount of material in the atmosphere be affected? Will it continue to change over time or become steady? Decide how to set and adjust the inputs to simulate the use of this energy resource. Record your reasoning as well as your decisions.

• Think about a third resource or a combination of resources. Decide how to set and adjust the inputs to simulate this energy solution.

• Test the model, and then decide whether you're satisfied with the way you're using the model. Adjust the simplifications or the way you set the model parameters, if you wish, but use the same approach for all three situations. Finalize your input sets.

HS-ETS1-4: Model the Impact *continued*

Using the Model

- Test the model to learn what it can do. Identify the inputs and outputs. Look at the range of each, such as the maximum and minimum possible values. Identify some of the factors that are interrelated, such as factors in feedback loops. Think about the strengths and weaknesses of the model.

- For outputs, look at qualitative results and at sequences as well as final outcomes and measurements.

- Make at least one test to determine how best to record the model's results. Look at what varies the most and record these outputs. Look at readouts and at any visual or other qualitative depictions. How will you describe or account for them? What about outputs that change as the simulation runs—will the final outputs be enough, or will you need to describe intermediate outputs?

Getting the Most out of "The Greenhouse Effect"

- Inputs for this model include greenhouse gas concentration and cloudiness. However, the gas concentration is qualitative for most situations. The three color-coded settings show that the slider is not linear. The cloud variable also does not produce a linear effect, but you can estimate the amount of cloud cover for each setting.

- Before you decide on the inputs to keep constant, explore the range of each input. Try the preset inputs (Today, 1750, and Ice age) and different Greenhouse Gas Concentrations. Try varying the clouds, the thermometer setting, the photons, and the model speed. Record the possible ranges and your choices.

- For some inputs, you might want to test several options rather than keeping that input constant.

- The temperature readout is one output. However, you are not limited to temperature. You can pause the animation to sample the photons at different altitudes. To explore the radiation budget, you can watch the photons enter and leave at the top.

Presenting Results

- Choose a way to present the model inputs and outputs. For example, you might present the inputs that you kept constant in a table or a screen shot, and then use a table or graph to present the changes.

- If you prefer to think in scientific terms, you might treat the inputs that change as independent variables. However, your alternatives might not isolate the variables, as in a science experiment. For example, a change from gasoline to hydrogen fuel cells might stop the increase of CO_2 (a greenhouse gas) but would increase the amount of H_2O. Water is a greenhouse gas and also affects cloud formation, so several variables would change.

- For this challenge, you had to make simplifications. Record the simplifications that you made. Discuss how those simplifications may have limited your results. For example, in the model, clouds are treated as an input. In the real world, water is part of several feedback loops. When clouds form, the water that condenses into cloud droplets or crystals is no longer acting as a greenhouse gas. The system is complicated and difficult to model, and so choosing the simplifications is part of the process of modeling.

HS-ETS1-4: Model the Impact *continued*

Extensions

- Carbon-containing emissions are not the only factor in determining the amount of CO_2 in the atmosphere. Organisms on land and in the ocean remove CO_2 through photosynthesis and add CO_2 through respiration. The ocean can absorb and release CO_2, depending on temperature and on the amount already absorbed. Organisms in the ocean incorporate CO_2 into shells and other structures. But CO_2 makes water more acidic. Too much CO_2 can kill the organisms that remove CO_2 from the air and water. Temperature also affects the organisms. In other words, the feedback loops can be complex. Decide whether (and how) to take these effects into account in your model inputs. Simplify, but be aware of your simplifications.

- If you modeled clouds, think about extremes, such as consistent clouds or ice ages. You can use Earth's geological ages or other planets as ways of looking at these extremes. For example, the greenhouse effect on Venus is so strong that the planet is covered by clouds. Temperatures do not change much between day and night, and they are much more consistent from pole to equator than the temperatures on Earth. For a cold extreme, think about ways to use the clouds in the model to simulate ice cover.

- Think about more realistic models. One international goal is to make changes in human activity in order to keep global warming below 2°C (compared with the 1990 average). International agreements often center on reducing greenhouse gas emissions. Some agreements focus on a target date for the peak of greenhouse gas emissions, after which the rates will drop. However, reducing greenhouse emissions is not the same as reducing the total amount in the atmosphere. "The Greenhouse Effect" doesn't allow you to set numerical values for the greenhouse gases, but you might find a model suited to the modeling of international goals.

Engineering Design

Science is a way to study the physical world. Engineering design, in contrast, is a way to achieve practical ends. Both approaches often involve data, mathematics, and computational thinking. Both rely on evidence and often involve models. Both involve asking questions and solving problems. Scientific activities focus on asking questions to develop explanations, whereas engineering activities focus on defining problems to make changes.

USEFUL CONCEPTS IN ENGINEERING

In engineering, design is the purposeful or inventive arrangement of parts of details. It makes use of the ideas below. If any terms are unfamiliar, look over the appropriate section before reading about design cycles.

- criteria and constraints
- benefits, costs, and risks
- tradeoffs
- testing, troubleshooting, and redesigning
- systems: components, inputs, outputs, controls, and feedbacks

Engineering Design

ITERATIVE DESIGN CYCLES

Engineering design, like scientific inquiry, is based on a set of practices that are used in different ways. Engineers often use a method of repeated, or iterative, design cycles. The designs are possible solutions to the problem. During the iterations, a design is chosen, refined, and implemented as the solution. This method can be roughly divided into three types of activity:

- **Define** Determine the problem to be solved and its important details.
- **Develop** Plan ways to solve the problem—select or create designs.
- **Optimize** Test and evaluate the solutions and refine the most promising solution(s).

The first iteration, or design cycle, typically starts with a definition phase, followed by development, and then (usually) optimization. Additional cycles follow and may involve different sequences or combinations of these activities. For example, several cycles of optimizing might be followed by a new plan, a new definition of the problem, or separate cycles for additional problems. Sometimes an idea does not work out (or does not work out soon enough). In such a case, an engineer might develop new possible solutions or reconsider solutions that had been discarded. Sometimes the problem needs to be redefined. Sometimes a plan involves breaking the problem into smaller pieces. In the latter case, each of the smaller problems should be defined.

Use this guide as you define and solve an engineering design problem.

DEFINE THE PROBLEM

Think of your engineering problem as a situation that you want to change. When starting a new engineering project, first define the problem. For example, you might want to prepare food or plan a trip. When the problem has already been defined—perhaps from a previous design cycle—it is still a good practice to review the problem.

| Engineering Design *continued*

You can define a problem by characterizing the criteria and constraints involved. Think about the conditions that a solution to the problem must meet to be successful, such as satisfying a group of specific needs and wants. Record those conditions as *criteria.* Think about any conditions that might limit or restrict a solution. Record these conditions as *constraints.* (You will find more detail in the section below about criteria and constraints.) For example, you might want to prepare food because a neighbor grew more vegetables than she could use and gave you a share of them. The criteria would include preparing the vegetables you now have. A constraint might be to use all of them while they are fresh.

You will use these criteria and constraints as you develop one or more designs to solve the problem. Some properties of a design, such as its price or the amount of time it takes to implement, may depend on the specific design. Your criteria may be to minimize these properties, to maximize them, or to match ideal values. Constraints can be requirements to stay within a range of values. Sometimes a constraint relates several properties, such as when the total price of several items must not exceed a budget. Whenever reasonable, quantify the criteria and constraints—describe them through numbers or comparisons.

At times, it is not possible for a solution to meet all of the criteria while staying within all of the constraints. At other times, you may need a solution so quickly that you cannot consider all of the criteria and constraints. In these cases, you may have to determine which conditions are more important than others, or what types of compromises you will accept. To identify these priorities, you might use labels such as *required* and *desired, acceptable* and *ideal,* or a numerical rating or ranking scale. You may find it useful to prioritize your criteria and constraints even if you think all of them can be met. Priorities can help you find a good solution faster by letting you focus on a simpler problem at first.

If a problem is complicated, you may be able to break it into smaller problems that you will solve separately. Sometimes you can separate small, connected problems by allowing each small problem to produce criteria or constraints for other small problems. As a result, you may need to solve some small problems before others.

As you define a problem, you may have to decide what to leave out. Real-world problems take place in larger systems. For example, a plan for lights for a school would likely involve the school's electrical wiring system, which could affect other electrical equipment. You can be distracted by all of the connections, and it is often wasteful to spell out all of the possible conditions. Instead, choose the conditions that are most important to test or confirm. Then group the rest of the connections by using a general statement or two, such as a constraint that the solution will not produce negative impacts. For the lighting-plan example, you might have a constraint that changes will not cause problems in the electrical system or other equipment.

DEVELOP A PLAN OR DESIGN

Research the problem and explore the possibilities. You may need to study the details of the problem or different aspects of the systems that are involved. As you generate possible solutions, you may need to find out even more specific information about the problem or the systems. You might even need to model or test the system to get necessary data. For example, you might map a route or use a trip calculator to determine the range of possibilities.

| Engineering Design *continued*

Review the solutions and processes that people have developed for other problems. It can be easier and less risky to adapt an existing solution than to invent a new solution. For example, it is usually easier to use or adapt a recipe than to invent one. Existing solutions have already been through cycles of optimization, so many of the component problems and issues have already been resolved. The effects of the solutions, including unintended consequences, are already known. You might be able to choose the best of several possible solutions, you might adjust one solution to suit your problem, or you might combine parts of different solutions.

Generate or find multiple solutions or approaches. Use your knowledge and your research to imagine possible solutions. The first idea is not necessarily the best idea, so try to ensure that you have explored a wide range of possibilities. Sometimes an unworkable idea can lead to a better idea. After you have generated a good set of ideas, use the criteria and constraints to evaluate the most promising ones. The use of criteria and constraints can help you be objective, especially when evaluating your own ideas.

Usually, designs alone do not provide enough information to produce the best solution—you need to test one or more solutions. Plan your approach for testing and optimizing. You may need to test and compare several solutions. You might find that one solution shows the most promise, but that you will need to test different settings or other details. The number of solutions and variations you test depends, in part, on the costs of each test. If testing is easy, you might be able to perform many tests. If testing has high costs or risks, you might use research, thought experiments, and calculations to reduce the choices. Or you might use a simple test or model to explore the feasibility of a solution or to gather data to adjust the properties of a solution.

OPTIMIZE THE SOLUTION(S)

You have many approaches available to find a good solution and adjust it to best suit your particular problem. You might test a real solution on the real situation, such as when you try a recipe or walk a planned route. This approach will usually give you the most reliable information, but it is not always reasonable to do. You may be able to test a sample of the solution, such as by cooking a small amount of food or by timing how long it takes you to walk a short distance. Often, you can test a solution by using one or more models. As you know, there are many different types of models to consider. You might combine sample data with a model. For example, you might use a friend's experience of walking your planned route, but adjust the time to reflect your own walking speed.

Test, evaluate, and refine your solution(s) iteratively. These cycles of optimizing your design are often when most of the work takes place. In the first cycle, you might narrow your choices to one main solution. In later cycles, you might refine different details of the design, such as the component pieces or the inputs to a system, to improve the performance or outcome of your solution. Tests and models can also help you clarify a problem or discover a new aspect to the problem. You may not be able to control as many of the factors as you would in a science experiment, but make your tests as systematic as you can.

❘ Engineering Design *continued*

Multiple Solutions

You might have several solutions to test, such as several cooking methods for a vegetable or several types of transportation for a trip. Apply each solution to your problem to find out how well it fits the criteria and constraints. Suppose you wanted to evaluate the amount of time needed for each solution. You might cook a sample of the vegetable using each method, or you might consult recipes to estimate the cooking time using each method. For a short trip, you might try each possible mode of transportation, or you might use an online trip planner to estimate the travel times.

These tests might also give you information about cost, ease of use, or other properties of the solutions. If one property is important enough to form the basis for a decision, you might make a single type of test. If several properties are important, you might need to make several types of tests.

Results can be complicated, such as when one solution is the fastest but a different solution costs the least money. You may need to make tradeoffs. You might find it helpful to rank or rate the time, money, and other factors. A chart that shows rankings or ratings may help you evaluate the solutions and see the possible tradeoffs clearly.

Details of a Solution

Sometimes, you need to test a solution just to see if it works. More often, though, you need to test different details of the solution. For example, you might test different power settings for microwave cooking or different times of day for a bus trip. In some cases, it works well to treat these variations as if they were different solutions, such as making the trip in rush hour or in the middle of the day. In other cases, you might explore how a factor affects the outcome (how two variables are related). For example, you might cook samples of food at low, medium, and high settings, evaluate the results, and estimate the best setting. You might then perform another set of tests at that setting and at settings slightly higher and slightly lower. In this way, you could optimize the power setting.

Troubleshooting

Sometimes a design does not work or is not reliable. You may need to try different ways to fix the difficulty or failure. You might study the difficulty as a new problem. These activities are called troubleshooting and are somewhat different from refining a design to improve it. You might find that that the difficulty cannot be prevented, but that you can reduce the effects. You might find that a design cannot be fixed or is not worth fixing. In such cases, plan a new solution or go back to your definition of the problem.

Unintended Consequences

Imagination and models can help you predict the outcomes of a solution but are not always complete enough. Solutions may have unplanned outcomes—good, bad, neutral, or mixed. When you are able to make a test of the real solution on the real problem, you are most likely to discover such unintended consequences. At times, you might test a solution or model in extreme conditions or continue the test until something breaks to determine the likely consequences of failure. You can also observe solutions similar to your solution to raise your awareness of possible outcomes. You might ask someone familiar with the problem to review your design or tests and identify possible consequences. You might adjust your criteria or constraints to take these effects into account.

Engineering Design Concepts
CRITERIA AND CONSTRAINTS

In science, you typically define a problem by identifying the variables and constants. In engineering, you typically define a problem by specifying the criteria and constraints. Criteria tell you the conditions for success, such as meeting specific needs or wants. Criteria might include a need to eat something nutritious and a wish for it to taste good, or a need to travel to a place for an event. Constraints tell you the limitations involved, such as cost, reliability, and the safety of people, property, and the environment. Criteria and constraints can go beyond science to include the interests of communities, cultural values, and aesthetic choices. They might include long-term effects as well as initial outcomes. They might require a solution to include ways to address any unfairness or reduce any harm.

Sometimes a condition can be stated as either a criterion or a constraint, such as the condition that food be nutritious. It may be easier to group criteria and constraints rather than to classify each condition as one or the other.

When you state criteria and constraints, think about how you will test solutions for success. When measurements, counts, or comparisons are useful, specify them. For example, you might specify that the price must be less than $10. But be ready to question and restate these conditions as you design solutions. If you obtain a discount or share expenses, the price might be greater than $10 while the amount you pay is less than $10.

BENEFITS, COSTS, AND RISKS

A *benefit* is an advantage resulting from a solution. A *cost* is a disadvantage and may include anything you give up or use up to achieve a goal. A *risk* is the possibility of suffering harm or loss—an uncertain cost. Some factors affect others. For example, a tightrope walker accepts the risk of falling, but a safety net can mitigate the cost of falling. Some factors may change over time. For example, small amounts of money, or of heavy metals in the body, may be negligible for any one event but may build up with repeated events. It may be difficult to predict some factors. Other factors may not be apparent until after a solution is implemented—a solution may have unintended consequences.

TRADEOFFS

In science, most of the problems you have encountered have exact solutions. In engineering, you instead seek to design the best solution for the criteria and constraints. You evaluate tradeoffs as one way of determining which solution is best.

A *tradeoff* is the exchange of one thing for another, such as when you give up a less-important feature for one that is more important. A tradeoff can also represent the balance among the needs and wishes of different people or groups. Tradeoffs usually apply to solutions and may reflect priorities. One solution might involve an increase in cost to improve time—that is, the solution would cost more but take less time. Another solution might do the opposite: it would cost less but take more time. You have to decide which tradeoffs to make. When you try to get the best value for the money, you are deciding on tradeoffs.

| Engineering Design *continued*

TESTING, TROUBLESHOOTING, AND REDESIGNING

In science, you might isolate a single issue to understand it. In engineering, you must take into account the consequences of your design, even if you do not understand all of them. Testing and troubleshooting help engineers account for unknown factors. For example, engineers may perform tests and then use statistical methods to take into account the variation or uncertainty. To reduce risks, an engineer might add a margin of error or might design for more extreme conditions than those measured or expected. An engineer may use an estimate rather than an exact value if the result is good enough for a design. An exact value may be determined later or may not be needed.

As in science, engineering tests can involve real materials and situations, models of many types, and combinations of the two. However, engineering tests typically focus on comparing a solution with criteria and constraints and then making a small adjustment and retesting. Sometimes a different solution or a large adjustment is needed. These changes are part of redesigning and optimizing a solution.

Troubleshooting involves locating and eliminating sources of trouble, such as fixing a broken part. Sometimes the trouble cannot be located. For example, a failure may occur only sometimes, and the engineer may not be able to reproduce it reliably enough to study it. The engineer might adjust the design to affect the most likely cause or might take steps to mitigate the failure if it occurs again.

SYSTEMS: COMPONENTS, INPUTS, OUTPUTS, CONTROLS, FEEDBACKS

In science, you identify independent variables, dependent variables, and constants. You may have classified these factors as givens and unknowns. In engineering design, the situations are often complicated and it might not be possible to know all of the factors involved in a problem. For example, a variable might start out as independent but then be affected by other factors in a complex way.

An engineer may look at a problem in terms of a system or of interacting systems rather than in terms of variables. It is not always necessary to understand all of the details of a system. In many cases, you can treat a system as a "black box" by looking just at what goes into the system and what comes out, or the inputs and outputs. For example, you could view a factory as a black box that takes in raw materials and energy and puts out products and waste materials.

When you want to have a little more detail about a system, you might look at the parts of the system and at how they interact. Two useful ideas are controls and feedbacks.

Controls are a way of adjusting, on purpose, how the system works. Suppose you have a system in which a microphone is connected to a combined amplifier and speaker. The volume adjustment on the speaker is a control. You use it to adjust how much the system amplifies the sound—how much louder it makes the sound.

Feedbacks also adjust the system, but come from the system itself, usually from an output. If the sound from the speaker is picked up by the microphone, that sound is amplified and reproduced by the speaker. The resulting sound is also picked up by the microphone and increases the sound from the speaker. As a result, the sound grows louder and louder. Feedback is called positive when it tends to increase a change, as in this example. Negative feedback tends to reduce a change, or return a system to its previous condition. Negative feedback usually makes a system more stable because it opposes change. Where feedback exists, a variable can start out as independent but then become dependent as well.